There Is

by Tameron Dennis
illustrated by Eva Vagreti

Core Decodable 4

McGraw Hill Education

Bothell, WA • Chicago, IL • Columbus, OH • New York, NY

MHEonline.com

Send all inquiries to:
McGraw-Hill Education
8787 Orion Place
Columbus, OH 43240

ISBN: 978-0-02-145147-0
MHID: 0-02-145147-8

Printed in Canada.

9 10 11 12 KOD 24

There is a .

jacket

There is a 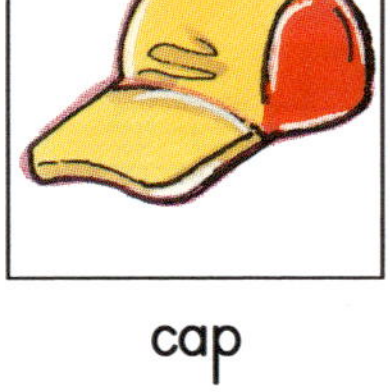 .

cap

There is a  .

backpack

There is a .

lunchbox

There is a .

book

There is the .

bus